# cold.

*Untamed Beauty*

---

Cold isn't always winter,
but winter is always cold.

# Other Works

*Motherhood: The Crucible of Love*

# cold.

### Untamed Beauty

dominique m. snedeker

---

Published by Hear Our Voice LLC

First Edition of this book was published November 2022 by
Hear Our Voice.

ISBN

Publisher
Hear Our Voice LLC
www.hearourvoicellc.com

Cover Design and art: Dominique M. Snedeker

Fonts Amsterdam Two, and Kenao Sans Serif licensed through
Canva Pro, 2022.

*To the One who formed us for*
*Work and for rest,*
*Who tethered the seasons and*
*Orchestrated their dance,*
*It takes my breath away.*
*I see your fingerprint*
*In leaf veins, and*
*Your creative Glory*
*In the sequins of the stars.*
*I hear*
*Your terrible rumble*
*In the power of the wind.*
*Though we may not understand*
*Your kindness,*
*and we misperceive*
*Your ways,*
*Your creation reflects your mind.*
*How can this majesty reflect anything but a*
*Good God?*

# Contents

# Preface

As a military family, we move according to the needs of the Air Force. As it turned out, the Air Force wanted my husband in North Dakota, and so we moved, from temperate Seattle-like Germany, to the frigid tundra of doom: Minot, North Dakota.

When I was a Lieutenant, I was haunted by photos of large semi-sized Air Force trucks surrounded by roof-high snow. Stories trickled down to my base in Wyoming (where snow blows away instead of sticking), of roads in Minot so packed with snow that those same semis would get stuck for hours, unable to turn around until rescue equipment could dig them out. Stories of snows so high you could crawl out your second-story window and stand upright. Stories of horror and dismay.

So as a veteran and mother of two toddlers, when the orders came, my husband dragged us to this horrible Narnian place where it is "always winter but never Christmas.[1]"

Ha.

---

[1] C.S. Lewis, "The Lion, the Witch and the Wardrobe"

I'll admit that I've lived in places where it *is* cold. Colorado Springs gets pretty nasty with its high altitudes; Wyoming and Montana have freezing winds that never stop blowing. We know about cold.

But not cold with toddlers.

My first experience in a whiteout, of Laura Ingalls repute, was with my two babies in the back seat. We were exploring our new town in late March, when suddenly it started to snow. It went from clear to a wall of white in twenty minutes, and I drove the highway from mid-town to base, at five miles an hour or less, praying the whole way that we wouldn't get stranded and die. It was a mercy the little ones slept. I didn't even have blankets or extra food (we were such newbs) but the thought of stopping somewhere didn't occur to me until it was too late to turn back.

Cars skidded on either side of us but I pressed on, hoping I wouldn't go off the road in our blindness or ram into spun-out cars. My husband waited anxiously for two hours for us to drive fifteen miles. I couldn't call him to say we were okay; if I had looked away from the few inches of visible road, I would have become disoriented. When I finally texted him in the parking lot of our base lodging, he rushed outside in relief to help me carry our boys through the weather into the snug little hotel room. We have never experienced sheer terror like that, with our two sleeping children in the backseat and death on the horizon, and I have never again left for anywhere in winter season (also meaning fall and spring) without first checking the forecast.

For those of you who live in cold places, you understand the necessity of having a vehicle (and house) full of everything—gas, blankets, toys, chargers, clothes, food, water, flares. You also understand that our lives are dominated by the constant threat of cold.

For those of you who have not yet had the pleasure of frostbite or lived in the threat of dangerous weather exposure, I want to invite you into our experience.

In this book, I explore the nature of cold in context of time, temperature, seasons, location and people, how cold affects our daily lives, mind, culture, and surrounding landscape. Cold can be personified or seen as just the temperature. Cold often causes the metaphor that needs exploring.

For more context, at the time of writing, we were at the tail end of reopening after COVID-19, and at the beginning days of the Russian invasion of Ukraine in February 2022. See what you see in these poems, that is the beauty of the art.

However, I hope to take you on a journey of shock, frustration, respect, pleasure, and satisfaction as I settle into life in Minot. I want you to feel the temperature changing, see the beauty of the spring fields recently watered by melted snow, and sense the vexation, isolation and joy of a frozen landscape, or delight with me in an ice cube on a hot summer's day.

Cold isn't always winter, but winter is always cold up here in North Dakota. I hope to draw you into an examination of what cold feels like to a transplanted mother of (now) three in a place where cold matters.

And we families of the more extreme latitudes (or altitudes) want you to know that there is beauty, glory even, in these winter places.

*Out of the inner parts shall a tempest come, and
cold out of the north.*
—*Job 37:9 DRB*


*Out of the north comes golden splendor [and
people can hardly look on it];
Around God is awesome splendor and majesty
[far too glorious for man's eyes].*
—*Job 37:22 AMP*

# cold.

*Untamed Beauty*

---

# Introduction

*—Why not Minot?*
*—Freezin' is the Reason!*

The saying goes back to a short-lived baseball team in 1917, and yet, the chant has become a part of the identity of the city, appearing in slogans, social media, and news articles, even as the rodeo bull *Why Not Minot?* It can mean good things of potential, or can dismissively accept the status quo. Like a tagline, it identifies the common memories of the inhabitants, whether recollections of a historical blizzard, or the snowstorm on, no joke, May 17-18, 2022.

The threat of a sudden cold-front is just a part of everyday life, and that sense of survival creates an instant intimacy between folks as they emerge from snow drifted homes to slide all the way to work or buy some diapers. This is a community of survivors.

Unlike most places in warmer climates, North Dakota doesn't shut down in wintertime. Schools are open; stores are open. People don protective winter clothes and go about their days, business as usual.

The cold is not a leisure experience in North Dakota, although there are moments when the humidity is high enough that the snow sticks together to form balls. This is not recreational snow, no choppers dropping daring snowboarders down mountainsides. No, nothing exotic like that. We plow our driveways. We push through uncleared roads. We get to school and work on time. This is survival. We live this.

Although this poetic work is centered on Minot, North Dakota, its themes sweep across the northern (and some very southern) latitudes and higher altitudes. People from epic places like Afghanistan, Ukraine, Scandinavia, Canada, and the surrounding states like Montana, Wyoming, Minnesota, and of course South Dakota (incredibly beautiful with a lot more trees) to name a few, will recognize some of their own narrative in these poems. An Icelandic woman found her story in "A Winter Quarantine."

To give backdrop for these poems, let us set the stage with some facts. A quick internet search reveals that North Dakota experiences continental weather patterns affected by the Alberta Clipper which causes rapid weather change, and the infamous El Niño which brings milder weather and La Niña, more extreme.

The average annual temperatures don't tell an accurate story when you look them up.

Those don't include windchill, or how cold the temperature feels to a living thing. In our time in Minot, and we're talking Fahrenheit, we have experienced -60 °F windchill and have read our thermometer at a whopping -27 °F below on the way to drop a toddler off at preschool. My truck started reluctantly that morning.

The other factor that creates an intense climate is the temperature swing. Last winter we recorded -26 °F and this summer it got up to 101 °F. That's an incredible 127 °F difference in just a few months. If you want to discuss how it actually felt to us, the numbers get a lot wider. In a single day the weather can swing 50 °F or more.

Yet another reason why we don't pack away much of our winter gear: SNOW! The only two months it hasn't snowed in North Dakota are July and August. In the United States, this extreme variance of temperatures is only bested by Montana and Wyoming, and only after North Dakota, does Alaska show up in fourth.[2]

Like its neighbors to the north and west, there are not a lot of trees to block wind or to protect from snow. We're talking prairie, flat rolling country formerly populated by buffalo grass as tall as a horse's shoulder and herds of

---

[2] https://www.earthnetworks.com/blog/swing-states-americas-extreme-temperature-ranges/

bison which are now replaced by farmland and tractors.

Within this world of flat, windy, extreme cold, I would like you to discover what it means to be stuck in a storm, or in your house for long periods of time.

I would like you to see how long winter lasts, because even after the season has ended, it is never far from thought. In a place where winter is hiding behind every corner, we're always on the lookout for cold.

# An Invitation

I am not just the poet
Sitting here
Exploring the
Wind
As it bites my fingers and nips my ears.

I am not just the poet
As the
Leaves shift colors before me and
My eyes observe the
Fierceness of the storm.

You, too, are the poet as
Words fly at you, as
You catch them and order them in
Your mind.

You are the one
Imagining in the
Spaces between words,
Forming shapes into meaning.

When I say cold,
I mean the sensation on my skin,
But you might mean the feeling in
Your heart.

When I say storm,
I see lashing snows and rains.
You might think of
Life and all it throws at you.

I am not just the poet,
Watching the glory of
Life unfolding before me, who
Dictates the every who, what and why.

You are the poet, too, as
You read the words and
Let them shape and
Reshape
You.

# Part I.

## Unexpected Tyranny

# Nerves Unraveling
(as evidenced by rhyme)


I cannot see the road.
Wipers anxiously slash
Back and forth,
Back and forth,
Back and forth but they
Are bound by ice.
>    *Thunk.*
>    *Thunk.*
>    *Thunk.*
Snow blows across the road
Sideways, fast—furious.

The wind is angry, again.
The snowflakes are
Yanked against their will,
And I cannot see the road.

The blowing heat is warm, not hot.
I shiver in the cold. My fingers
Clutch the wheel. I still cannot
See the road.

My tires slide—the road is slick,
The car beside just spun.
My babies shriek—I ease the brake
Oh, where is that blessed road?

I crawl forward, gently now,
Inch one, inch two, inch three,
The wipers *thunk*, the heater fails,
Panic stabs at me.
Oh God, there goes another car,
Oh please, I cannot see!

Oh Father God, please answer me,
And show me where to go,
My babies in their car seats be,
I must, must see the road.

The wind pauses in its rage,
The snow falls down instead
Of blowing dense and thick across
I see *the road ahead!*

Snailing inch-by-inch and mile-by-mile
We wait for moments to flee.
I'm shaking now, my nerves are
Shot, but the road, sometimes,
I see.

"What took so long?" He rushed at me
With arms out warm and wide. Grabbing
One, I hand him one, each child we rush
Inside.

I start to whimper, my breath is bound,
For fear has stolen me,
Arms draw me back and then I sob:
"We only *almost* died."

Winter storms do not play games,
They murder and they maim.
The Lord took mercy on our lives,
And got us home again.

Cold.


Light reflects off of mounds
And piles, and drifts of
Snow.

Endless waves of white,
Like a sea, or more like a
Desert—
Dangerous. Barren,
Monotonous.

The wind shapes—
Sometimes like fingers in clay,
But
In storms it whips
Its victim in fury.

In the morning
Sun glints off
White,

Endless white,

Waves
       and waves
             and waves
                  of empty

Cold.

# Winter Quarantine

My heart aches. The difference between
Leaden sky and
Leaden land
Is a faint erasure lining the
Horizon.

Each burrowed home is a
Kingdom deep unto itself—
Huddled figures, if at all,
Scoop wildly until mounds,
Bulwarks really,
Surround and then delete the
Inhabitants.

From my frosted window the forlorn wind
Vocalizes my torment,
And seeing nothing but
Gray,
I rush out to scream with the howls—

But the sound chokes in my throat.

    I gasp

    As the

    Cold

Steals my voice.

Fiery darts of ice
Prick my skin,
Chasing me back into
My prison

And I deflate—
Spent—
Sliding down,
Down,
Down

Into the
Darkness of the

Night.

# November Wails

Shrieking wind lashes itself
Against the windows and
Eaves of my house.

Its furious howls make
The house tremble in fear—
In submission. For on the morrow
It will be the only house whole
Without shingles or siding
Gone flying on the wind,
Riding high and fast like witches.

My house trembles in the angry
Tempest holding fast against the
Maul—the scorn of something
Uncaged, wild, unbound
Mocks, threatens and flaunts its power—

But my house remains,
Solid in the cold, its foundation
    *Deep,*
    *Deep,*
    *Deep*
Underground.

It will not fail, for it contains
Three sleeping treasures within.

# Is It Only February?

Hot tea,
Hot bath,
Hot sauce,
       Anything
       But
Wind shrieking,
Pounding
Smashing,
Howling in my eaves—

Cold wind,
Cold skies,
Cold ground
      Everything
        Is
Freezing,
Slowing,
Stilling,
Even in our minds—

Flying off into nothingness,
          The gray-white nothing
      The white-white nothing
            The heatless nothing
          In the endless
      Fields
  of
White.

# Icefields

Monochromatic monotony—
Meandering miles of
Shifting,
Shivering,
Swishing
Frozen
Ice

Skitters in
Shuddering,
Shaking,
Stuttering
Cold.

Lonely.
Isolated.
Alone.

# -26° With a Windchill of -51 F°

Between yesterday and today,
It is fifty degrees warmer.
But we're still living on the knife's edge.

Just because it's fifty degrees up
Doesn't mean that you can't
Still freeze to death in the
Wind and the cold.

> It's like living on a moonscape.
> I need a spacesuit to keep
> My children safe.

Yesterday my truck
Barked and coughed and
Spluttered and choked when
I started it.

Today, with drifts still thigh-high
And dazzling light blinding me
She started right up—It's
Fifty degrees warmer,
And Yet

22

I am
Still
Surrounded
By
Cold,
Endless
Snow.

# Agony

The fire abuses my skin,
The fire of
Cold and ice.
Shrieking tormenter of
Lost souls, or people struggling
To their cars, into their homes,
Wind, you foul witch, you
Angry fiend,

Why do you rage?

Sometimes you rest,
Your breathing gentle,
A sigh lifting bees in flight.

Sometimes your soft kiss
Sweetens the brow,
Mitigating the temper of the sun.

Sometimes you delightedly
Toss colorful leaves like
Confetti in your harvest joy.

What torment of soul
Makes you lash in anger,
Never pausing for a moment,
In rage and fury?

What ancient guilt?
What mournful sorrow
Overcomes you
As you thrash about
Destroying all around you?

Oh wind, oh gentle breeze
Be spent, let go, forgive.
Remember summer, or
Springtime or trees,
But if not,

You need to know:

Your wailings are the sound
Of many voices,
Lonely, afraid,
Confused.

But hope rises on the horizon,
The sun and moon you cannot change.
The Maker has a plan for you,
If you allow yourself home again.

# Part II.

Tug-of-War

# Thaw
(Ukraine)

There's a battle between
What's cold and what's not
As ancient as time itself.

Slowly, the warmth loses
And for a time, the white rules
With clenched fists and chaos.

But almost without notice
The what's-not stirs silently,
Creeping up slowly, carefully

On tender feet—at first
Only a memory, but soon
One brave drip inspires another

Till at once the chilly storm
Loses its teeth before the gaining
Torrent, and what once was frozen

Begins to thaw.

# March, April, May

The sound of drops,
Tiny stalagmites of cold, but
In reverse,
Diminishing quickly,
Instead of
Slowly expanding over
Time.

*Dit. Dit. Dit.*

Winter's tears or the
Perspiration of spring,
Drop all around—

The rhythm of
Juxtaposition,
Of collision—
(Delicate in dropperful drips)
Melodically splash the

Change of seasons,

*Dit. Dit. Dit.*

The sound of
Sunlight on ice is
Inconsequential yet
Portentous—

The tiny mouse that
Roars in like a lion
And out like a lamb.

# Spring,

Your promises of
Lazy clouds and cleansing rain
Are tricky.

Sometimes you are heavy and
Cold,
Your promises vague
Memories or words on the
Tips of our tongues—

Sometimes bright and clear
Like buttercups or Robins' eggs

And others muddled like
Puddles of melting snow and
Thawing mud.

We long for certainty—
No more guessing games or
Charades, or make-believe
When *we* carry the burden of
Faith. Are you finally here?

No, Spring, you promise big:
New Life. Renewal. What can get
Much bigger than that?
It foreshadows the biggest
Redemption of them all.
You promise hope
And the thawing of frozen
Hearts.

Spring,

We look into pools littered
With shards of last year's
Leaves and wind-torn twigs,
Sacrificed
For the sake of roots and
Future buds,
And we see our faces
In glimmers of sunlight
And cloudy shadows

Hoping to discern the promise
Of finally seeing
And being
Seen.

or to know
and to finally
be known

# The Underground

Back then
I shivered with anticipation—
Verdant Seattle beckoned,
Calling at first in mother's voice—
Trusted, peaceful,
But soon the energetic call of
Adventure
Rippled through my body.

Every
Single
Act of self-will
Converged
To keep me at
My desk, while the
Biology teacher
Dissected cool breezes and desire
Into temperatures, numbers, and
Dictionary words.

Wild things long for grass—
Wide open
Spaces of
Instinct—

Snorts and
High-stepping
Full-throttled
Speeds,
Zigzags
Course through bodies
Summoned by
Growth and
Sparkling sunlight.

Not so Dakota Spring—

When Winter contends
For Summer's divine right,
And in between there's thaw and
Freeze
And
Thaw
Again,

A cold, muddied,
Yellowed,
Feeble
Spring above,

But below,

In dark thawing earth,
A resistance sprouts,
Awaiting opportune time,

To triumph
In the
Sunlight.

# The Unveiling

The morning
Dressed in mist, in
Hovering fog, is
Undecided or
Unwilling to expose what lies
Innocently sheltered in
Cloud—

That same morning, inspired by
Technicolor sunrise and ancient
Hues of awakening
Time,
Slowly reveals the emerging
Treasure
Resting peacefully within—

Tiny shoots of green in yellowed
Grass,
Newborn buds nestled in stiff stalks,
And under our deck between supports,
A nest! A
Hopeful, newly-formed
Nest.

The morning chill, so
Cold it required parkas, begins to lift into
Sun-streaks,
Golden windows of
Royal light.

.

That feeling of potential rises inside
Like the morning damp
Dissolving
Into clouds that will
Fill
Drop by drop
To overflowing,
Returning
Again and again and again
To bring
Hope and life to
Earth

# Poetry of Rain

Windshield wipers toss the cold rain back
And forth like children playing ball,
The rhythm hypnotic,
The movement soothing to
Ruffled feathers and the
Sound of rain pitter-
Pattering—windy fingers—
Drumming cadences
That pace galloping hearts.

Those who care too much,
That love too much,
Who want too much
Sometimes find the waiting
Just a little too much.

And so—

The road.

# Crucible

You thought it might be
Over,
This whipping and scouring,
This
Frigid blast of heaven's breath.

For moments of hopeful
Chirps
And the innocence of green
Nestled
In dead-brown tangles of
Dried-out branches and roots

Gave you hope
That
This time of discipline,
Of
Pressure and molding
Just
Might be over.

Well, it isn't.

As
Long as you have breath
You
Will be enfolded in this process
Of
Times and seasons, of rest and
Growth,
And pressure, and scouring

Until,
Like cold marble you
Yield the secrets inside—

Like squishing clay
You
Expand or contract or
Expand again and again

Till you
Sparkle.

Till you
Shine.

Till you burst forth
Spring buds
With
Promises of
Fruit and
Harvest.

You thought it was
All over.

I'm sorry friend,

It has just begun.

# Lake Darling

Faded yellow fields
Ripple in the wind
Like the thawing lake
Teeming with returning geese,
Now laden, itself, with
Small crawling things
Emerging in the lack of
Cold.

Faded gray fields and
Frozen ponds
Burst with
Potential and
Life.

Sometimes there are
Secrets
Hidden
In those
We cast off as
Old and lifeless.

# Part III.

*Fullest Expression*

# One Thing Never Wasted

Sunny days—when people emerge from
Hibernation, and like hares,
Molt their winter wares for colorful
Sun-shiny things

Like lime, yellow, turquoise, and skin!
What a beautiful color is skin
Freed from its cavern of sweaters and coats.
Skin reminds us we are people, all of us and
Not coat-hangers or
Beds mounded with comforters and duvets.

No, the secret of skin is the sensation of
Life,
Freedom of movement,
Beauty of bright and heat—

Skin, the canvas of
Insect bites,
Grass hives,
Peeling burns,
Scrapes and scratches and
Glorious days of play—

Days full of
Lemonade with neighbors and
Crowded splash pads,
Long waits for ice-cream and
*I didn't know you were pregnant.*
*What a beautiful newborn!*

No one wastes the feel of wind caressing
Shoulders,
Or
Cold pool water on the smalls of sunburned
Backs.

Toes wiggle in grass or sandals,
Exulting in freedom like

The crowds of people,
Milling about,
Just to get a coffee, or
Hear a band.

The people! All the glorious,
Wonderful people beholding the
Green of quivering leaves, engrossed in the
Rumble of motorcycles and
Bicycles and skates.

No one wastes the light, or day, the time full,
Ever full of lunch dates, and playdates and
Actual,
Romantic, *where-are-our-kids?* dates,

Or late-night sunsets, and midnight campfires,
Nighttime bugs, and burnt marshmallows,

Sunshine-heat, bright colors, loud music,
Crowds, knees, construction trucks
(not plows)—
No,
Not one of us wastes our precious,
Lovely
Summertime.

# Reopening

Oh friends,
Are you getting into the rhythm of
Summer?

Of
Heat—
Big lazy clouds, and
Ice cubes
Clinking in your glass?

Have you gotten used to
Twilight nights
And salty days,
Flying watermelon seeds
And dusty toes?

Are you gathering inside
You every sunbeam
And sunburn—
All that sun-beaten heat
And sunlight?

Do you bask in green and
Blue and color so bright
Your eyes close against the
Glare?

These summer things.
These long, winding
Meandering days of
Freedom.

Hot nights and cold drinks.
Friends and neighbors.
Sound.
And smells.
Lots and lots of
Smells.

Yes. Friends.

Are you finding
Each other,
And what it feels like
To be part of a whole,
Or a group
Or community?

This is what summer
Feels like:

*Hope.*

# Enthalpy and Entropy

It's a bizarre circuit:
Animation and action
Cultivated by fierce
Stimulation
Punctuated by
Stillness.

Like aggressive heat
From searing sunlight
And days so dry that
Death hounds from behind
Until
     You
     Drop

     Into


     The



     Cold



     Pool,
     !SPLASH!
Or drops of rain pour frenzied from storm clouds
*Slap! Slap! Slapping* your face.

But again,
Animation returns
Like the heat,
Making you long
For the stillness
Of
Cold.

# That Passage of Time

Slow
Summer breezes over
Prairie grasses,
Bending gracefully
Like ballet dancers—
Trees bouncing in the wind—
That time,
That warm,
Sinuous sunlit
Time
Softly treading over
Shoulders and
Duckbills and
Grasshopper wings.
Summer
Time
Might be punctuated by
Thunderstorms        and
Cold,
Vehement        rain
But those storms only
Serve as relief,
A contrast,
A contrast        to remind us

Just how peaceful is

Flickering
Sunlight, and
Butterflies
Dancing in
Summer breeze.

# July

Warm twilight explodes
In manufactured
Shooting stars and
Thunder.
Bare shoulders touch
And small children
Nuzzle into laps.
Detritus of barbecue
And sparklers lay
Cool and then cold
While bright rain
Glitters down
In starlight.
Moonlight illuminates
Upturned faces
And damp eyes.
Despite the turmoil
This is a moment of
Unity.
And for that
We can give thanks.

# Luxury

Hot breath ruffles the lake,
A sunny kiss
On sandy footprints
And on brows
Mopped with sweaty curls.

This breeze lifts the shrieks of
Giggling sandpile builders
High into bilious clouds
In a cycle of joy that
Stuns me to silence

Only met by that
Pause
And then

Drop
Into
Refreshingly
Cold
Lake water.

As I emerge
Spluttering in
Exhilaration
I am met by
Windy kisses and
Sunny breath
On my shoulders and
I float in
    the
Loving embrace.

# Eighty-Nine

Eighty-nine degrees in North Dakota
Isn't sweaty.
It's neither swamp,
Nor soup,
Nor sunburn
Nor layers peeled and left
Crumpled on the floor.

Eighty-nine degrees in August
Is
Heavy wheat heads drooping lazily,
Buffalo grass waiving in harmony—
Feathery seed pods soft like vintage fringe
Hiding under flapping poplar leaves quivering
Shiny, like raindrops dropping in the wind.

Eighty-nine is an age,
Droopy, rheumy eyelids
Napping in the afternoon blanket of
Sunlight,

And it is a time—
When haystacks rest lazily to dry in the
Eighty-nine degrees of heat.

Gradients of blue fade into horizon white
Where yellow fields
Juxtapose with green.
High above, I know this looks like
Patchwork,
Like a quilt,
Like the earth is one giant hand-sewn
Picnic blanket

And maybe it is—

Fields of food waiting
For the more-than-summer
Tractors, and midnight harvesting before
The onslaught of
Angry clouds and
Freezing winds.

But for now, I will listen to the
Symphony of crickets and birds,
Of rustling grass and shivering leaves
With the sound of construction trucks
Lumbering past

In this moment of eighty-nine—
In this not quite yet cold autumn heat
Of final summer's day,
And the solitude of sunshine.

# Before Snow Falls

In the distance
Fields of green
Shimmer in the breeze

A giant green ocean reflecting
Sunlit heat and light.

The sound satisfies,
Swishing stems and stalks,
Rhythmic,

Hypnotizing,

As breezes toss
My hair and cool my warmed skin.

Time is either stopping or running through
Or maybe both,
Mesmerized, entranced
By this land ocean
Brimming with food—
Brimming with life.

There are no cold depths to this
Shallow sea and yet the mystery is there,
Hidden more in time
Rather than in depth.

Soon this vast green will become yellow
And then white. Soon the shallow will
Recede with the heat and the
Depths and mystery of
Monochromatic life
Will return.

# Part IV.

## Fly Away

# Cognitive Dissonance

When they tell me school starts in August,
I balk and then concede.
All sun-kissed children must return to
Desk, despite the heat.

The empty backseat is pleasantly quiet,
As we speed by cows on the left,
Except for the toddler bouncing his foot—
He's singing a song his bubbas taught him.

August is summer, isn't it? Why the
Silent splash pad, empty pool, and
Windblown swings?

I suddenly miss those ever moving
Noisemakers,
Yet the toddler ogling an ant has curls
Flashing in the sun, and I feel content.

For once, I have some time to
Drag the child, at our own pace,
Across grasses, under leaves,
Through shimmering sunlight,
Surrounded by green, golden flecks, and
Time.

But the prick on my skin feels cool—
Almost.

Cold creeps into the mornings, and I
Wonder if maybe they're right.
August is fall, after all,
In these parts.

# Oak Park

I love the feel of cool crisp mornings.

I love the color of almost-fall, of
Almost-the-leaves-changing-color, of
Anticipating that
Siennas and ochres and sepias will
Soon blush the mornings
As we walk through the brittle air.

That morning air—
Cool, brisk, tiny cold pinpricks
On my skin,
And as we walk, I
Observe the changing colors,
Imagination running wild as
Thoughts run loud and bright

Like

Friday night football games
Under flickering lamps, and salty popcorn
Teasing the nose, and the pulsing beat of
Drumlines, and voices lifting high into the night—
All that adolescent potential brimming over

Or of

Autumn nights—
Turquoise skies fading into
Midnight blues and
Stars so thick
They might melt on the tongue,

Or of

Cool mornings and warm sweaters and the
Shattering silence of crunched leaves
Under foot,
And that sweet,
Innocent,
Spicy
Hope
Returning with the smell of
Pumpkins.

I love the promise of autumn.
Every crispy breath soothes my soul, and
Gives me courage to face the cold.

# White Gulls

Shifting patterns of birds
Surfing the air
Circle—
Not a murder exactly,
But a colony of seagulls
Lost
So far inland
From their cold ocean winds,
That incessant chirp of
Grasshoppers
Orchestrate their
Erratic movements.

Like thoughts
Harassed,
Non sequiturs
In this endless landscape of thistle and
Wild wheat grass,
The white gulls search for perch,
For haven,

And having found
Similitude in the fierceness of the gale,
In the restless
Waves of grasses
Tossing ceaselessly,

Make the prairie their
Resting place
And eventually,
Their
Home.

# Midnight by Moonlight

The moon round, glowing and
Pregnant with starlight
Shimmers in the deepening lake.

Geese returning south slumber
Silently—an armada of sound and
Instinct in the morning cold—
But for now, they rise and fall
With the breath of the wind
As it flicks feathers and spoils
The waterscape echoing
The starry, starry night.

The waters, lulled peaceful,
Kiss the rocks and stones of shore,
And time rests in the arms of
The moon, caressed by the wind,
Enfolded in the silence of the night.

# Grandpa

Old hands rough with years and worry
Sitting idle, wishing for fingers clasped,
Long and thin, or thick and chubby—but
Hands that have since aged and faded
With the rise and fall of wanting,

Thumbs thick with dirt reaching into
The bowels of deep brown secrets of
Growing things and future hopes,
Now shudder, thick with ache and yearning.

Oh, winter-cold, oh twilight years
This slow descent into evenfall,
Into geese honking over lakes
Flying ahead of the winter storm,

He sits, with blankets draped or
Perhaps memories wrapped—
And waits in solitude, longing
For moonlit nights and dewy sunrise

For fat, sticky giggles, and long, low
Dulcet humming as she sews
Or sets the table, and that gaze—
Eyes clear with wintry blue.

Hands sit slow and quiet, lingering—
Remaining steadfast in remembrance.

And then those hands reach
For that tomato sandwich,
Cold and fresh
Like every summer past.

# October

What is that feeling of October?
September builds all month to this moment—

In coastal regions,
September is
New school shoes,
Novel possibilities and
Restless potential energy.

But here
In hotdish country, way over here in the cold
Tempestuousness of the northern plains,
September is
Autumn,
With school already well underway.

September is the wildcard, the joker, the
Unstable, double-minded, manic month of
Sunshine or
Snow or
Anything between.

Ah.

October
Is solid.

Its time is harvest,
Unmitigated—
For neither snows, nor heat
Can change the necessity for
Winter preparation.

October anticipates the cold while
Reveling in summer products. It is the
Haven for hues ripened on the vine, of
Leaves expiring in the wind—
The slow ascent into holiday season.

October winds,
Melancholy with sentiment or
Melodic with expectation,
Regardless,
Require an upturned collar at the minimum
And *that*
Can be counted on.

# Made for the Extraordinary

There is glory in every season,
Yes,
That quiet, bubbling excitement of
Spring,
That colorful rumble of
Summer sunlight,
Stark winter
In its emptiness,

But nothing is like the ocean of
Leaves, flashing by my boots,
Brown waves of skitter-scratches
Scattering in the breeze.

The cold from far off unknown places
Chills exposed fingertips—frozen nails
Slashing shallow scratches across faces,
Down spines.

But loosening, exhilarated hearts fly
High
With the gale,
Dangerous,
Yes!
But not deadly,

Each gust a breath in my lungs
Reaching down deep to my soul
Reminding me that

An ending too,
Is a beginning,

And seasons'
Passing
Is part of life.

And that I,
Yes, I
Am epically,
Gloriously,
Furiously

Alive.

# Riding the High Wind

Leaves scratch against pavement,
Wind tossing orange waves,
Not in a steady pendulum beat,
But instead, following some ancient rhythm,
A heartbeat of freedom, of
Daring, riding whiplash
Just ahead of the cold winter storm.

Piling the ground, almost like bodies, rest
Copper leaves, purple, sienna, auburn—
Some green, some new
Right off the
Branch
Ripped loose in their
Prime by the insistence of the
Wind.

Time has come for all;
The seasons stop for none,
But all can ride the windy currents and
Rise up on the shoulders of the storm,

Lift high in the violence of the wind,
Flying away
In an autumnal
Blaze of glory.

# Grasshopper's Fiddle

Do you not hear it?
Does it not call to you,
Echoing somewhere between your
Courage and
Dream-space?

I yearn to wander, to
Follow whispering leaf songs—
Susurrations of
Yellowing grasses and rusted leaves
As they gather *en force* on
Melodious brooks, that hint in their tinklings of
Distant chittering pine needles, and the
Staccato crashing of
Cold seas on ancient rocky islets,

To places forlorn, of which,
I have yet to
Inhale the essence.

I ache to undertake
Long desperate journeys
To oaken lands on elven shores.

What calls to me in the whisper of
Windswept plains and river wood?
What thrums my heartstrings until my
Blood beats with this indiscernible desire?

Do you feel it deep in your chest, in that
Cavern containing unwhispered dreams?

The leaves loosed in the tempest,
Flying off heroically to certain death
Contest
That tenuous hold on me of
Hearth and home.

Kindred with claims deepest,
Ancestral,
Tether my feet but
Yearning stretches my imagination
Taut

While desire fiddles on my back
As my hands prepare one-by-one
And two-by-two for hibernation.

# Part V.

Finding Home

# Too Late

It comes when least expected,
As leaves flaunt their doomed colors,
Tenaciously clinging for one more day to
Branches already prepared for cold,

As children rush to recess under a
Sincerely optimistic sun,
As shoppers push carts, backhoes dig,
As road workers signal "SLOW,"
It comes.

It comes when most anticipated,
An awaited sneaker wave on coastal shores,
The sandy haboob lumbering towards small
Desert villages—a wall of breakneck change so

Rapid that seasons
                    exchange

And

All at once
Winter
Is
Here.

# Winter

You judge me by my
Shrieking in your eaves,
But have you ever thought
It might be your ill-equipped house at fault?

Oh. I'm cold. I know.

I've heard your names for those
Deemed cool and heartless, before.
They're not nice. And frankly, hurt my feelings.

I work for never ending months to
Freeze your ground, which I might add,
Reduces
Many of your unwanted bug populations—

I layer your fields with white
So that your happy
Little green shoots
Can flourish in that
Other "season,"
                 oh yeah
*Summer*.
I'm misunderstood in the job I do.

I pour out my love in white instead of
Green—I make high places low and
Low places high, soothingly
Smoothing the surface, imagery of
Some far-off distant prophecy yet to be fulfilled.

And,
        and,
                and

I give you time for rest.

You sleep under the blanket of
Stars.
You put down your shovel and
Pick up your fiddle

While I sing wildly of the cold and
Frozen starlight.

You huddle inside together, interlocked
Families finally reconnecting for warmth, or out of
Boredom, or for comfort. Who cares why.

You misunderstand my every whim,
My every fancy, and
Overlook my creative designs and patterns
I lovingly etch onto your windows.

I am overlooked most of the time for
Christmas, and I get that,
I really do, for
He who released me yet restricts me to
Time and season,
He—yes,
He came to this earth.

I decorate in celebration,
But you often curse me
Instead of noticing my handiwork.

I don't gather you to my bosom
Like that *other* season.
I know I would hurt you if I gently
Caressed you
Or dappled your skin.

I hold back as best I can—

So,

Look unto yourself,
If you burn under my touch.
Did you carefully prepare for it?
Did you heed my warnings and all the clues
I dropped?

Don't blame me for your own
Choices.

I am only a season
But you,
You
Are
Human.

# Blizzard

The house is full—
Too many bodies
Jammed like sponges,
Erupting out of their confined
Spaces into
Mine.

Their energy is like overripe
Tomatoes
Splitting thin skins
To ooze
Life, like Legos, which never stay
In the box,
Ever.

Confinement—walls and floors that
Stolidly remain cluttered with
Books and parts of toys and
Mail—

I cannot escape.
They cannot escape
This Isle of
Refuge.

For the storm is screaming,
Clattering our windows,
Fingers plunging into crevices of
Caulking that barely holds.
With manacled hands
It shakes the very frame,
The very heart inside of me.

*Don't break, don't break—*
*They are safe inside—the*
*House will hold.*

This refuge—this Island of Hope
Mocks every step,
Every turn—the same,
Same—
Walls, the
Same—
Same—
Same faces, the
Same,
Same,
Same,
Same mess—

And I wonder as I reach for
Chocolate, a book, my
Baby—
Anything—

If I will hold together
Long enough.

But then—

            —it stops.

                  I pause
Mid-step and
            listen.

Below, they watch the same
Mindless thing; above
I am
      alone.

It is quiet.

Jacketed,
           I push open the door.

Crisp, cleansing

Cold

Burns my lungs, and

I gulp

Deeply the needles and
Fire of

Cold,

The cleansing fire,

And as starlight and moonlight
Create dazzling snow-light,
Brilliant flecks dance on my
Horizon till it meets the sky,

And I
Breathe in

*Freedom.*

# The Answer

Before me, white open spaces span
So wide anything could happen.

The brittle air breaks in my throat,
Cold shards catching before melting
And washing my lungs clean.

The stillness of the air and
Intransigence of hard-packed snow
Tunes my senses as

Myriad sunbeams reflect off
Tiny crystals, each one perfection,
And my breath dances like smoke.

The air bites playfully, like a nipping husky;
Shocks of cold on my cheeks and wrist are
Almost like fingers prodding me after a joke,

And I get it!

From every surface—
Light.
From sky to horizon—
Light.
Bright light, daylight, sunset, then
Starlight—

From up above—
Light.

Billions and billions of burning stars reflected in
A billion, billion flakes of freezing
Cold,

And I hug myself in
Wonder,
At the
Vastness,

At the glory of it all.

# Forecasted Blizzard

*Dear. Get home quick. Storm coming. Can you get me...*

First year:

Milk—4 gallons
Eggs— 2 3 4 cartons
Bacon—3 packs
Apples—dozen
Carrots—3 bags
Celery—2 packs
Oranges—bag
Granola bars—3 boxes
Doughnuts—dozen
Crackers—6 boxes
Cookies—5 boxes
Cold Gatorade
Soda
Flour
Sugar

Pancake mix
Beans
Ground beef
Taco shells
Shredded cheese
Shredded lettuce
Coffee
Salt
Chocolate chips
Cake mix
Wooden spoon
Paper
Crayons
Toilet paper
Paper towels

Third year:

Milk—2 gallons
Eggs—2 cartons
Bacon—5 packs lol/jk
Apples—5
Celery—bag
Carrots—bag
Maple Syrup
Sweetened Condensed Milk
Food Coloring

Fifth year:

Milk—2 gallons
Eggs—1 cartons
Chocolate chips

Tenth year:

Creamer

# Snowscape

Endlessly perfect. Smooth.
White.
Pure.

Roads and mud,
Trash, and yellowed grass
Hide deep beneath the
Great and equalizing
Powder.

Even. Bright. Reflecting
Light, sunlight,
Blinding yet
Shining
Like diamonds and pearls.

The unmarred snow
Covers the sins of
Spring and summer and fall.

The snow,
Clean,
Silver, glistening
Will be pushed and prodded
By snowplows

And soon evidence will appear
Of the cold offenses of
Humanity.

# Sometimes, Winter Comes Softly
(a cold rhyme for Gramma)

No more with teeming flocks of life,
But now in slumber rests beneath
Cool blankets of effervescent white,
Existence reclines at last in sleep.

No frenzied colors buzz with noise,
But sweetly sings the softened blows,
And gentle does the wind caress
Existence in its soft repose.

Oh, gentle white, oh pure dawn day,
You morning sun, you starlit way,
I won't forget the lesson learned:
For wintertime, the earth has yearned.

# Womb

I love that pressed-in feeling of
Warm, tight walls—thick arms
Sheltering all the laughter and cookie baking,
Homework, and skating thick-soled woolen
Socks across mopped floors.

I love that tea-mug feeling,
That white cocoon outside
Silencing voices and distractions, and that
Scrunch of snow boots,
Almost like leaves, crunching underneath.

Burrowed down deep in our caves,
Each other for warmth,
Each other for laughter, even
Bickering, we
Nestle like puppies,
Like family—We are
Layers and layers of blankets,
Crumpled mixed-up on the floor,
Tangled and bungled but
Together nonetheless,
Sheltered by the
Cold,
Winter
Storm.

# Ice, Sixteen Inches Thick

Snow
Drifting swiftly like racers across the

                                 hardened lake
Then disintegrating like cold    breath    in
                         Glittering
Air,
        Reflects the floral hues of
Sunrise
          and

                      sunset
As the wind frolics to the music of
        Whispering snowflakes,
    Like          sand     shuffling
Together, like tinkling bells, like laughter,

Like the sound of starlight echoing down,

And the moonlight's maternal embrace.

# Cloaked Fields

Homochromatic hills,
Wide winning, shifting spaces
Of subtlety, of small,
Similitudes that speak to the
Soul, not of bland,
Boring
Spreads, but of
Secrets, waiting to be
Sniffed,
Sussed,
Spotted
In the
Crispy
Cold,
Brimming underneath,
With
Life.

# Hibernation Song

Rest a while in winter's long embrace,
Put down your plow and pick and sword.
Take refuge in the cold warmth of silence—
Lacework of frost and blankets of snow.

There's no time for strife or fighting or foe
For winter's night calls all to bed;
Slumbering deeply—a pause for peace,
And rest for the weary, burdened head.

# Fingerprints

Brown skeleton branches silhouette
Against the blank canvas of
Snow-packed earth and wintery sky.

For days, sun-thaw has crisped the top and we
Crunch and crackle through the crust to
Squelching snow beneath.

Weeks before, frost adorned the limbs in
Frozen diamonds;
Nothing manmade could ever echo the
Opulence of inspired ice. No queen
Could ever be so lovely as those frozen trees.

Soon, snow will thaw, beading pearls
Along seams of bark, hanging from
New shoots, from buds like cold opal studs.

Then mud will suck at our boots,
Slush shushing under our wheels,
But hidden beneath all the yuck,
Will be glorious, transient green.

Who can fathom the mind of the
One who turns death into life and
Fashions the delicate light to
Dance on frozen water,
Draping the seasons in epic glory?

# Perspective

Snow they said.
A huge cold front moving in.
Internet and news anchors
All abuzz with forecasted
Blizzards in
*April.*

At first, we laugh,
Then complain,
Then laugh again, when,
After three days in the
Belly of the whale,
We discover three, four, five
Foot drifts,
But pleasant temperatures
Above zero,
So our children are
Safe to play in the
Storm.

As ridiculous as it seems to
Celebrate Easter in
Snow pants,

We realize Winter's
Parting gift is to
Water the
Seeds of
Spring,

And thus the
Shoots of
Harvest
Unfurl deep in the
Moistened earth,
Ready
For their
Appointed
Time.

# Winter's Lullaby

I sing over
Wind swept plains—of
Things deep inside,
Resting,
Until the
Fullness of time.

Snowbanks and hoary frost hide
The gems, the
Jewels of seeds and things
Not yet in due season.

I sigh the howling wind,
Burying the secret things in
Blankets of snow,

And

I dream—with the seeds—of
The coming time
When
Awakening
Covers the earth.

# Epilogue

We were made for cold;
Maybe it was made for us.
Despite its danger,
Nothing like cold quite hones our focus,
Gives perspective,
Points us faster
Towards the
Hearth and
Heat of
Love.

Cold's touch burns—yes,
But so does the sun's,
And sometimes the gentle kiss of chill
Shivers excitement,
Its breath lifting us high,
      Up,
      Up,
Into the stratosphere, into
Another dimension—
      Up,
Into the heights,
For which we were made.

In a place where
Stars were made for plucking,
Our voices join the chorus of
Many waters,
The sound of life returning to earth, of
Thawing hearts, and
Tears,
So precious, every one is
                        counted,
Every one is
           saved—
That's the place of stardust and starlight,
The place which moves us down gently again,
Into the bosom of the earth,
To rest,
Just for a little while,
Until that
Glorious Day.

# Acknowledgements

This book was conceived almost as a joke between my publisher, Stacy Brevard-Mays and I as we worked on *Motherhood: The Crucible of Love*. The wind howled in my eaves for days as I edited and worked the *Motherhood* final manuscript. When I had enough of the house sounding like it would fly apart, I wrote a scathing poem about the wind. She loved it. I wrote another. And so it goes that suddenly, I had a book. I have to thank her for taking another chance on me.

My creative editor, Pamela Falkner, has a fantastic critical eye and having poured over this manuscript multiple times, she expanded and then focused my vision. In "Nerves Unraveling" she played with me, throwing changed rhythms, a different rhyme, words helter-skelter into the poem as I quickly pulled *some* of them out again. What was left behind is a well-laid poem. Had she not played catch with me, you might have gotten a second draft version. But also, for all the work and insight on all the other poems, too, thank you for so much of your brain and time. I've never debated one line in a poem with someone for five days, or gotten fifty subtitle variations in five minutes via text at midnight. Quite honestly, you make me a better writer with all of your word and logic challenges. I couldn't have done this without you.

I asked Erica Boivin to read, edit, and give feedback on the book. Right between two back-to-back evening concerts, she scrambled into the car (on her phone) to read and respond to the manuscript. Our conversations over some of the debated words or phrases were very enlivening. Also, a big thank you to Arvids, who hollered ideas from the background. I appreciate you both.

Over many phone conversations, Thelly Hudson helped brainstorm words and poem titles. The night before my final manuscript was due, she debated with me over a newly written addition, probably at midnight, after a long day at work, and debated cover strengths at ungodly hours. I enjoy your creativity. You're up next to chase your dream.

To my proofreader, Charlotte Turner, who saved me, you rock mama. A week after having a baby, you were still able to find typos and things my eyes smoothed over. Thank you for such a sacrifice and for making this shine.

Thank you, Kirstin Mueller, for being my grammar police. Oxford commas are our friends. I understand, I really, really, really do!

A huge thank you to Naomi Stearns for final-proofing and using your eye to spot anything out of the ordinary.

Hannah Lamar, you inspired some rhymes. Thank you for your feedback about structure. You are very right that structure holds the narrative together.

Erin P.T. Canning of the wonderful *Life Beyond Parenting Blog* and *Parents Who Write* podcast, your gentle feedback steered me in the right cover art direction. Soon after, ta da! Plus, all of our other fun conversations. www.lifebeyondparenting.com

Once again, thank you to the hive mind of Moms Who Write Facebook group who talked cover art www.momswhowrite.org. If you're a mom, and you write, please join. They are full of opinions, tips, ideas, experience and encouragement. And also, a little bit of fun.

Minot Moms Facebook group gave me good feedback on the subtitle, and voted on two covers I subsequently scrapped four hours later. Thank you, local moms, for your opinion. I took it all to heart. I hope you feel represented in this book and maybe find your story in here as well.

143

A special thanks to Mikayla Jade, who gave me great feed-back as a local in Minot. Your perspectives were invaluable and actually started a five day-debate between Pamela and I over a poem that I eventually pulled and replaced. Thank you for your critical thinking. I think it made this work much better.

A thank you to Chandell Lattin, for a midnight conversation about titles. Check her writing out at www.dellalattin.wordpress.com.

Roy Leavitt, your sermon at Open Gate Church on 10-17-22 clarified some of the themes I have been swirling around in this book. God made us with extraordinary plans in mind. He never made us for boring lives, but has put hopes and desires into our hearts to guide us to those epic things:

> Ephesians 2:10 TPT
> We have become his poetry, a
> re-created people that will fulfill
> the destiny he has given each of
> us, for we are joined to Jesus,
> the Anointed One. Even before
> we were born, God planned in
> advance our destiny and the
> good works we would do to
> fulfill it!

Dad, Andrew, Meera, Ron, your quick answers helped me make the decisions I had been laboring and deliberating over for hours.

Carl, my ever patient and practical husband. Thank you for keeping the boys out way too late just so I could have a quiet space to work this final draft. Your own input helped shape a better intro and preface. I think you've got a secret literary gift, but I won't tell anyone. Love you.

Royce, Landon and Garrett, my shining snowflakes, my wonderful boys, thank you for inspiring me. Royce and Landon, thank you for distracting the baby so I could work. Garrett, thank you for taking Mommy on walks to Oak Park where so many of these poems were written via phone while I pushed a stroller while you crunched leaves beside. You helped Mommy so, so much.

To the One who has inspired it all and is calling us all upwards and higher, you know how I feel. I am thankful you have opened my eyes to see, my ears to hear, and sped my fingers to respond.

If I forgot anyone, please forgive me. If you helped in any way, thank you, thank you.

Minot and North Dakota, thank you for becoming home. You have been a wonderful place to put down roots, and really, I know Christmas comes once a year; I don't think you're a place of doom; and I kind of really like you. If we have to move again (military life) we'll always have *cold. Untamed Beauty,* and, I will really and truly miss you.

# About the Author

Dominique Snedeker is a United States Air Force Academy graduate with a Bachelor's of Science in English—that wasn't a typo—veteran, military spouse, and mom to a house full of boys. When she isn't finding shoes, or cleaning up spilled milk, she's cooking and reading—yes, at the same time. Dominique currently lives with her husband and three boys, in Minot, North Dakota.

Dominique's debut poetry book, *Motherhood: The Crucible of Love* released April, 2022, explores the existential crisis of every parent adjusting to selflessness, sleepless nights, and special moments. Stay tuned for *Motherhood: Empire of Lost Toys and Mismatched Socks* in spring, 2023. Keep track of her and other upcoming projects at www.dmsnedeker.com.

©2020, Amberleigh Muehlebach Photography

Made in the USA
Middletown, DE
24 November 2022